REVISE GCSE

T0346093

REVISION PLANNER

Planning your GCSE revision:
A step-by-step guide

Authors: Rob Bircher and Ashley Lodge

Also available:

Revise GCSE Study Skills Guide
9781292318875

Full of tried-and-trusted hints and tips
for how to learn more effectively, the
Revise GCSE Study Skills Guide gives
you techniques to help you achieve your
best – throughout your GCSE studies
and beyond!

**For the full range of Pearson revision titles across
KS2, 11+, KS3, GCSE, Functional Skills, BTEC and
AS/A Level visit:**

www.pearsonschools.co.uk/revise

Contents

How to use this book

The aim of this book is to help you put together your **revision timetable** for your GCSE exams. This is a way of planning your time so that you cover what you need to for each subject you are doing.

Think of this book as a mini-project to put you in control of your revision. Feeling in control dramatically reduces exam stress.

Unlike a lot of school books, you really need to work through this book page by page – for parts 1 and 2, anyway. That's because it is a **step-by-step guide**. Each page will give you something to do or something to find out or think about. We've done it that way because you need to have a few things sorted before you can put together a really good revision timetable.

If you think this all sounds like it will take ages, don't worry. The time you put into completing your timetable will be time well spent. Your revision will be more **effective** and, because you'll have it all organised, revising will seem **easier** too. You might even find that you have a bit more **spare time**!

Icons used in this book

 = work with your wall chart

 = work with the planner sections in this book

 = write something into this section

 = copy this template to use for different subjects

 = information about how long a section will take

 = reward yourself with a treat

An example of how to fill something in.

Advice based on real students who have sat real exams.

❀ Mindfulness

How mindfulness practice might help you.

Student tip

Ideas on revision from previous GCSE students.

The revision route

This diagram explains the route that you'll follow in this book.

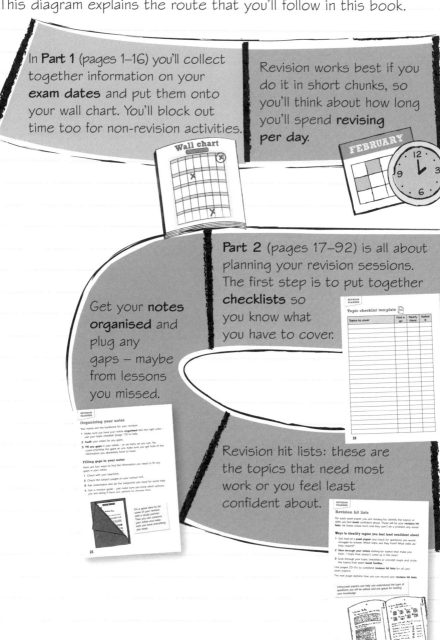

In **Part 1** (pages 1–16) you'll collect together information on your **exam dates** and put them onto your wall chart. You'll block out time too for non-revision activities.

Wall chart

Revision works best if you do it in short chunks, so you'll think about how long you'll spend **revising per day**.

FEBRUARY

Part 2 (pages 17–92) is all about planning your revision sessions. The first step is to put together **checklists** so you know what you have to cover.

Get your **notes organised** and plug any gaps – maybe from lessons you missed.

Revision hit lists: these are the topics that need most work or you feel least confident about.

The next stage is about working out your **revision time**.

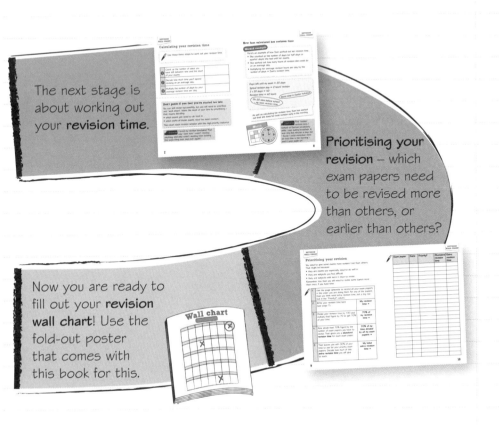

Prioritising your revision – which exam papers need to be revised more than others, or earlier than others?

Now you are ready to fill out your **revision wall chart**! Use the fold-out poster that comes with this book for this.

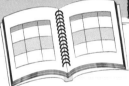

Now you are ready to plan what to cover in each session and set your revision targets. Use the **planner section** in this book to do this.

Part 3 (pages 93–103) of this book introduces some top **revision strategies**: try these out to make your revision more effective and enjoyable.

Part 1: Setting up your revision wall chart

Part 1 is about setting up your **revision wall chart**. This is the fold-out poster that comes with this planner.

When you see the wall chart icon, it means you need to do something with your **revision wall chart**.

Revision wall chart

Your revision wall chart:
- ✓ marks out your time for revision
- ✓ gives you an overview of your revision
- ✓ gets your revision in the right order.

It should take a maximum of 2 hours to work through this section.

Finding out when your exams are

Knowing the dates and times of your exams will help you to plan your **revision wall chart**. Some students put all their effort into revising for their first exams. This can leave you under-prepared for later exams. Planning your revision wall chart helps make sure you give each exam the right amount of focus.

Your teachers will have all the information you need about the dates, times and locations of your exams.

 Student tip Start revising as early as you can! That way, if you find something difficult, you have time to work it out or find help.

1

Write your exams here in date order. Use pencil first. Also include the deadlines for coursework or other non-examination assessments (NEAs).

Date/ time	Subject and paper	Location (which building / room)	My target grade

Now add the dates to your **revision wall chart.** You could use a red pen or a red sticker so they stand out.

What are your other commitments?

Before you complete your revision wall chart, you need to block out times when you know you are already busy.

This could be for a sports club that you go to every week, a visit away to see a relative, music lessons, band practice – other commitments.

Your teachers may set you homework while you are revising, so consider blocking out time for that as well.

How do I find out about other commitments?

Are there any family commitments over the revision period that you might not be aware of (or have forgotten about)? These are often recorded on the **family calendar**, if you have one.

There might be some commitments you can skip because you are revising for your exams. But it is good to keep a few things going during your revision time – **especially exercise**. Otherwise you can easily get 'revisioned out'.

Telling other people about your revision

Make sure your family know when you are revising, so they can keep out of your way and let you concentrate.

Do the same for friends so you can **minimise distractions**.

It's a good idea to clear all commitments during the weeks when you are actually taking your exams.

Write the other commitments you have during your revision time here.

Commitment	Day and time

 When you are done, block these times out on your **revision wall chart**. Use a different-coloured pen or highlighter, or stickers, to show that you won't be able to revise during these times.

Get a family member to check this list and remind you of any commitments you may have missed.

What's your study routine?

A routine is when you do the same things at the same times each day. A **revision routine** is a good thing to develop because it helps you **stay on track.**

Some people work best first thing in the morning; others take a while to get started and work best late at night.

When do you work best? Use this knowledge to help your routine.

 Use the space below to describe a successful revision day.

- When would it start and finish?
- How long would the revision sessions and breaks be?
- When would you have meals?
- When would your best times for revision be?
- What times of day do you find it hardest to concentrate?
- When would be the best time to build in an exercise session?
- How many hours of revision time are there in total?

Chunking your time

Research shows that we all focus better and feel more motivated when we **break tasks down into chunks.**

For revision this means:

- revising for 20 or 25 minutes, then having a 5-minute break
- varying the topics you are revising.

These things will make your revision more productive.

Once you have done two or three chunks, give yourself a longer break – half an hour, for example.

Here's an example of how a GCSE student called Chloe chunked her revision time after school:

16.00–16.30:	Relax/snack
16.30–16.55:	Maths – circle theorems
16.55–17.00:	Break/check phone
17.00–17.30:	Science – moles ☹
17.30–18.00:	Tea!!
18.00–19.00:	Homework
19.00:	Relax!

Student tip There is a huge amount to learn in a GCSE – it can seem hard to know where to start! Don't be put off. Just start at the beginning (of your Revision Guide, notes, etc.) and take a small chunk at a time.

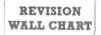

Calculating your revision time

 Use these three steps to work out your revision time.

1	Count up the number of days you have left between now and the start of your exams.	
2	Decide how much time you'll spend revising on an average day.	
3	Multiply the number of days by your average revision time per day.	

Don't panic if you feel you've started too late

You can still revise successfully, but you will need to prioritise and 'work smart'. Make the most of your time by prioritising – that means deciding:

- which exams you need to do best in
- which parts of those exams need the most revision.

Then start each revision session with this high-priority material.

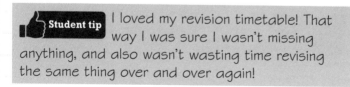

Student tip I loved my revision timetable! That way I was sure I wasn't missing anything, and also wasn't wasting time revising the same thing over and over again!

How Sam calculated her revision time

Worked example

Here's an example of how Sam worked out her revision time.

- She counted up the number of days (or half days or quarter days) she had until her exams.
- She worked out how many hours of revision she could do on an average day.
- Multiplying her average revision hours per day by the number of days = Sam's revision time.

Days left until my exam = 20 days

Typical revision day = 2 hours' revision

2 x 20 days = 40

Revision time = 40 hours

More time in Easter holidays

Do 20 mins before school - my best revision time.

As well as calculating her revision time, Sam has worked out that she does her best revision early in the morning.

March

Student tip Find 'hidden' revision time. I looked at German vocabulary while I was eating breakfast. It was only five minutes a day, but I found I could remember more at that time in the morning — and it soon adds up!

Prioritising your revision

You need to give some exams more revision time than others.
That might be because:

- they are exams you especially need to do well in
- they are subjects you find difficult
- they are subjects with more in them to revise.

Remember, too, that you will need to revise some topics more
than once, if you have time.

1	Use the page opposite to record all your exam papers in the order you are doing them. For any of the papers that you think need extra revision time, put a big red tick in the 'Priority?' column.	
2	Write your revision time here (see page 7).	**My revision time =**
3	Divide your revision time by 100 and multiply that figure by 70 to get 70% of your time.	**70% of my revision time =**
4	Now divide that 70% figure by the number of exam papers you have to revise. That gives you a **standard revision time** for each exam paper.	**70% of my time divided by all my exam papers =**
5	That leaves you with 30% of your time to use for your priority exam papers. Decide how much of this **extra revision time** you will give to each.	**My total extra revision time =**

Exam paper	Date	Priority?	Standard revision time	Extra revision time

Filling in your revision wall chart

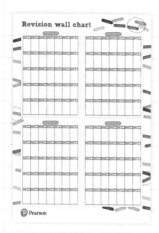

Revision wall chart

Pearson

Now you can add your revision time to your **revision wall chart.**

- Everyone's revision is different. We've left the dates blank so you can fill them in to suit when you start your revision.

- Each day on the revision wall chart has a maximum of five revision 'slots'. The lines are faint so you can combine slots together if you want to. Make sure you fill in breaks and free time as well as revision!

- Stickers – people use these in lots of different ways. What works well is using one colour for each subject or each kind of event.

What's the point of the revision wall chart?

The **revision wall chart** can:

✓ help you cover what you need to in the time you have

✓ allow you to prioritise subjects that need more revision

✓ enable you to use your time effectively

✓ spark your motivation to get revising

✓ let you know if your revision is on track or not.

Once your **revision wall chart** is up on display, you just have to follow it – simple!

Use the guidelines on the next page to get started.

'A stumbling block can also be a stepping stone.' This means that facing up to a challenge often turns out to be just what you need to get on track to success.

Revision wall chart guidelines

1 What should be on your wall chart already?

   a All your exams – check you've got them on the right days.

   b All your other commitments – block that time out.

2 You know what your revision time is for each paper – now you can slot that time into your revision wall chart.

   a Start with a priority exam paper – one that needs extra revision time or has exams early (see page 10).

   b Work backwards from the day of the first exam. You will want to spend half a day (or more) revising that paper either the morning before the exam (if it is in the afternoon) or the day before – so block out that time now.

   c Now use the rest of your revision time for that paper, putting in a chunk here and there as you work backwards through the wall chart, until all the time is 'spent'.

   d Do the same thing for all the top priority/early papers.

   e Then move on to the rest of the exam papers until all your revision time is used up.

Use a pencil or an erasable pen – revision plans can change.

It is a good idea to vary your revision chunks so you cover different subjects through the day.

Try scheduling your toughest subjects so they come first in the day. That way you'll be tackling them when you are fresh.

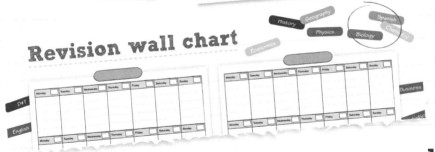

Revision wall chart

Rewards

Staying motivated is really important. A good way to stay motivated in your revision is to:

- set yourself **targets**

- **reward** yourself when you hit your targets.

Setting targets

It's a good idea to set a **target** before each chunk of revision. For example: to complete a topic, to condense three pages of notes or to answer an exam question under timed conditions.

Remember to make your targets achievable and realistic.

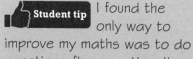

Student tip I found the only way to improve my maths was to do question after question. It was hard at first, but after a while, I began to understand how the questions worked.

Planning rewards

Reward yourself when you hit your targets. You'll need to think about what rewards would work best for you. Some ideas might be:

- **Small rewards** for hitting a revision target, such as a 5-minute break, a chunk of chocolate, listening to a favourite song.

- **Medium rewards** for completing all of your targets for a day or for the week, or after each exam, for example a cinema visit, a gaming session or a night out with friends.

- **Large rewards** once all your exams are over, like a holiday or time out with friends.

Planning your rewards

 Plan some realistic **targets** and **rewards** here.

My target	My reward
Small	
Medium	
Large	

Your first **reward** should be for completing your **revision wall chart**.

What will your reward be?

Reviewing your revision

You might not feel like you have time to think about your revision as well as doing it, but research shows that taking a little time each day to review your revision really **helps you remember more.**

- Start each revision day with a 5-minute session thinking about what you want to achieve that day.
- Spend 5 minutes at the end of your revision for the day reviewing what you have done.
- Make a list of what you plan to cover next.

Reviewing your revision wall chart

Now you have finished Part 1 and have completed your revision wall chart. Well done!

Take a few minutes now to review your wall chart.

- Fix any little mistakes or problems with it.
- Research says it is a good idea to think about challenges ahead, as this helps you deal with them. So if there are some tough-looking days ahead, face up to them and think of ways to tackle them.
- Taking the time to complete Part 1 is an important achievement. You have taken control of your revision, which also means getting a grip on exam stress.

> Experts agree that students who have a revision timetable (and stick to it) usually do better in their GCSEs than students who do not.

Student tip For my French speaking exam, I learned phrases I knew would always be useful, such as 'in the background', 'on the left of the picture', 'in the middle of the picture', 'it seems as if'. I had them ready to use – no matter what the picture was about!

Space for reflection

 Use this space to record your thoughts on your revision. Think about how you will tackle any challenges.

Part 2: Planning your revision sessions

What do you need to revise?

Part 2 is about planning your revision sessions. You'll do this in the **planner**: the section of this book that looks like a diary (pages 59–90).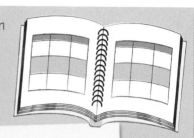

A revision session is the time when you sit down to do several chunks of revision. It is **important to plan** them so that you:

✓ cover everything you need for each paper

✓ know what to revise each day

✓ stay focused on your targets for each session.

It should take a maximum of 2 hours to work through this part (if you already have topic lists for your exams), plus about 30 minutes a week planning your revision sessions.

Each exam paper you do has a list of topics and/or skills to cover. You can find these topics and skills listed in the **specification** for each subject.

It can be tricky to find the exact specification you are following, so it is much better to ask your teachers for a **list of the topics** you need to revise for each subject.

Then you can **put together a checklist** for each exam you are doing. There's an example on page 18. There's a blank one that you can copy as many times as you need to on page 19.

Worked example

History: Medicine in Britain, c.1250–present

Topics to cover	Had a go	Nearly there	Nailed it
c.1250–c.1500: Medieval medicine			
Supernatural and religious ideas about causes of disease	✓	✓	✓
Theory of Four Humours, and miasma theory	✓	✓	
Remedies, e.g. bloodletting, purging, purifying air			
Hospital care	✓	✓	✓
Black Death case study, 1348–1349			
1500–c.1700: Medical Renaissance			
Continuity and change: causes of disease	✓	✓	
Change: scientific approach (Sydenham)			
Change: influence of printing press/ Royal Society	✓		
Continuity in prevention and treatment: hospitals and community			
Changes in treatment: better medical training, influence of Vesalius	✓	✓	✓
Case study: William Harvey			
Case study: Great Plague in London, 1665			

Topic checklist template

Topics to cover	Had a go	Nearly there	Nailed it

Topic checklist – concept map

Some subjects have clear-cut sections, but others can seem more complicated, with topics connecting in different ways.

For these subjects, it may be easier to present your checklist as a **concept map** (you might also know them as spider diagrams or mind maps). You can find out more about making **concept maps** on page 97. Here's an example of a concept map for one topic from one unit of a Religious Studies GCSE.

Worked example

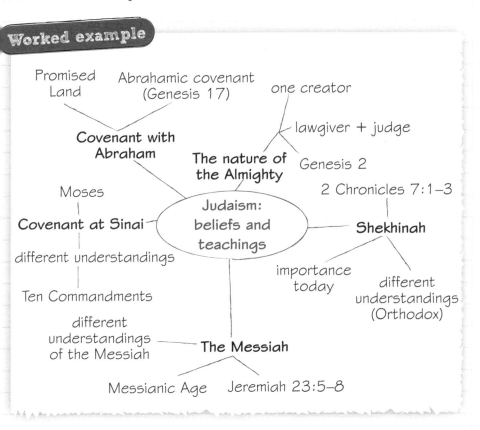

Promised Land
Abrahamic covenant (Genesis 17)
one creator
Covenant with Abraham
lawgiver + judge
The nature of the Almighty
Genesis 2
2 Chronicles 7:1–3
Moses
Judaism: beliefs and teachings
Covenant at Sinai
Shekhinah
different understandings
importance today
different understandings (Orthodox)
Ten Commandments
different understandings of the Messiah
The Messiah
Messianic Age
Jeremiah 23:5–8

Organising your notes

Your notes are the backbone for your revision.

1 Make sure you have your notes **organised** into the right units – use your topic checklist (page 19) to help.

2 **Audit** your notes for any gaps.

3 **Fill any gaps** in your notes – or as many as you can. You could prioritise the gaps so you make sure you get hold of the information you absolutely have to have.

Filling gaps in your notes

Here are four ways to find the information you need to fill any gaps in your notes.

1 Check with your teachers.

2 Check the subject pages on your school VLE.

3 Ask classmates who do the subject(s) you need for some help.

4 Get a revision guide – just make sure you know which options you are doing if there are options to choose from.

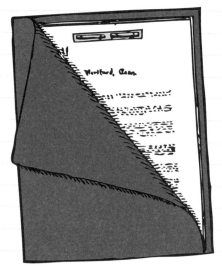

It's a good idea to do some of your revision with a study partner. Then you can compare your notes and make sure you have everything you need.

Gaps in my notes that I need to fill

Subject	Missing notes – description	PRIORITY

Revision hit lists

For each exam paper you are revising for, identify the topics or skills you feel **least** confident about. These will be your **revision hit lists**: hit these areas hard and they won't be a problem any more!

Ways to identify topics you feel least confident about

1 Get hold of a **past paper** and check for questions you would struggle to answer. Which topic are they from? What skills do they require?

2 **Skim through your notes** looking for topics that make you think: 'I hope that doesn't come up in the exam.'

3 Look through your topic checklists or concept maps and circle the topics that seem **least familiar**.

Use pages 25–54 to complete **revision hit lists** for all your exam papers.

The next page explains how you can record your **revision hit lists**.

Using past papers can help you understand the type of questions you will be asked and are great for testing your knowledge

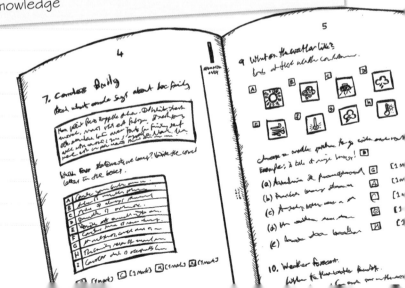

Worked example

Here's an example of how to use the **revision hit lists.**

Revision hit list: Science

Subject: Biology   **Exam paper**: B1: Influence on life

Top three target topics

Topic	What's the problem?
Genetic diagrams	Can't remember how to do these
Alleles	Just the whole thing! Need to get it straight in my head
Spread of pathogens	What are animal vectors? On past paper but...?!

Next five target topics

Topic	What's the problem?
Darwin + theory of evolution	Hard to remember all the different parts to the theory
Calculating ratios	For monohybrid crosses

Examiners' report

A key skill in Science exams is being able to apply what you already know to new situations.

Revision hit list

These pages are blank for you to fill in your own subjects.

Subject: Exam paper:

Top three target topics

Topic	What's the problem?

Next five target topics

Topic	What's the problem?

Examiners' report

Be sure to support your points with evidence from the text.

Revision hit list

Subject: Exam paper:

Top three target topics

Topic	What's the problem?

Next five target topics

Topic	What's the problem?

Student tip Create mini posters of key equations that you need to recall in your exam and put them next to the mirror in the bathroom so you can read/revise them while cleaning your teeth. This will improve your whole family's science knowledge, too!

Revision hit list

Subject: Exam paper:

Top three target topics

Topic	What's the problem?

Next five target topics

Topic	What's the problem?

Examiners' report

Make sure you have a good grasp of terminology so you
can be confident that you are using terms correctly.

Revision hit list

Subject: Exam paper:

Top three target topics

Topic	What's the problem?

Next five target topics

Topic	What's the problem?

Examiners' report

Make sure you consider why the writer has chosen
particular words, phrases or images.

Revision hit list

Subject: Exam paper:

Top three target topics

Topic	What's the problem?

Next five target topics

Topic	What's the problem?

Examiners' report

Set out your working in an organised way, showing the steps you followed.

29

Revision hit list

Subject: Exam paper:

Top three target topics

Topic	What's the problem?

Next five target topics

Topic	What's the problem?

Check through your answers – it's easy to make simple mistakes that could lose you marks.

Revision hit list

Subject: Exam paper:

Top three target topics

Topic	What's the problem?

Next five target topics

Topic	What's the problem?

It's important in Chemistry to know how to write balanced equations, using the correct symbols.

Revision hit list

Subject: Exam paper:

Top three target topics

Topic	What's the problem?

Next five target topics

Topic	What's the problem?

Examiners' report

Always read each question carefully. It can help to highlight command words, key terms and the number of marks.

Revision hit list

Subject: Exam paper:

Top three target topics

Topic	What's the problem?

Next five target topics

Topic	What's the problem?

Examiners' report

Revise the experiments you carried out during Science/ separate Sciences as well as the topics in the specification.

Revision hit list

Subject: Exam paper:

Top three target topics

Topic	What's the problem?

Next five target topics

Topic	What's the problem?

Examiners' report

Where you are asked to draw or complete a diagram, make sure you use a ruler for straight lines. This not only makes your work neater but it is quicker than drawing freehand and leaves no doubt about your understanding of the diagram.

Revision hit list

Subject: .... Exam paper: ....

Top three target topics

Topic	What's the problem?

Next five target topics

Topic	What's the problem?

A key skill in GCSE exams is being able to apply what you already know to new situations.

Revision hit list

Subject: Exam paper:

Top three target topics

Topic	What's the problem?

Next five target topics

Topic	What's the problem?

Examiners' report

If a question includes data, for example data presented in a table or a chart, make clear use of it rather than just referring to it in passing.

Revision hit list

Subject: Exam paper:

Top three target topics

Topic	What's the problem?

Next five target topics

Topic	What's the problem?

Revision hit list

Subject: Exam paper:

Top three target topics

Topic	What's the problem?

Next five target topics

Topic	What's the problem?

Some subjects, such as History, have the same sequence of question types each year. This makes practising these exams easier, but make sure you know exactly what the questions want your answer to do.

Revision hit list

Subject: Exam paper:

Top three target topics

Topic	What's the problem?

Next five target topics

Topic	What's the problem?

For subjects like Geography and Biology, practise drawing diagrams against the clock so that you don't spend too much time in the exam thinking about what to include.

Revision hit list

Subject: Exam paper:

Top three target topics

Topic	What's the problem?

Next five target topics

Topic	What's the problem?

Examiners' report

Learn, understand and be able to define the
key terms used in your course.

Revision hit list

Subject: Exam paper:

Top three target topics

Topic	What's the problem?

Next five target topics

Topic	What's the problem?

Examiners' report

In humanities subjects, you often have to prioritise your
reasons for something: so, as well as remembering factors,
you have to say which was most important, and why.

Revision hit list

Subject: Exam paper:

Top three target topics

Topic	What's the problem?

Next five target topics

Topic	What's the problem?

If a question asks you to use your own knowledge in some way, make sure you use it to answer the question – don't just write all the facts you can remember.

Revision hit list

Subject: Exam paper:

Top three target topics

Topic	What's the problem?

Next five target topics

Topic	What's the problem?

For languages, use vocabulary easily and naturally rather than forcing words that you've learned into sentences where they don't really make sense.

Revision hit list

Subject: _____   Exam paper: _____

Top three target topics

Topic	What's the problem?

Next five target topics

Topic	What's the problem?

In modern language listening exams, listen to the whole passage first rather than just homing in on individual words.

Revision hit list

Subject: Exam paper:

Top three target topics

Topic	What's the problem?

Next five target topics

Topic	What's the problem?

Every exam paper has important information about how to complete it on the front page. Make sure you understand this information and follow it carefully.

Revision hit list

Subject: Exam paper:

Top three target topics

Topic	What's the problem?

Next five target topics

Topic	What's the problem?

Managing your time is very important for exam success. Remember: allow around 1 minute per mark, and make sure you give yourself enough time for longer answer/higher mark questions towards the end of the paper.

Revision hit list

Subject: Exam paper:

Top three target topics

Topic	What's the problem?

Next five target topics

Topic	What's the problem?

If your subject has a theory section and a practical
section, you can often use what you've learned in your
practical work to help you answer theory questions.

Revision hit list

Subject: Exam paper:

Top three target topics

Topic	What's the problem?

Next five target topics

Topic	What's the problem?

Examiners' report

Always have a go at answering all the questions you need to answer.
Make sure you have enough time to finish the paper. Don't forget to
look on the back of the pages!

48

Revision hit list

Subject: Exam paper:

Top three target topics

Topic	What's the problem?

Next five target topics

Topic	What's the problem?

Examiners' report

Make sure you know the key terms for processes and can describe each step.

Revision hit list

Subject: Exam paper:

Top three target topics

Topic	What's the problem?

Next five target topics

Topic	What's the problem?

Make sure you know what the different exam question
command terms mean, e.g. *name, state, give, describe,
outline, evaluate* and *explain* (see page 99).

Revision hit list

Subject: Exam paper:

Top three target topics

Topic	What's the problem?

Next five target topics

Topic	What's the problem?

For any exam, the best advice is to read the question carefully. Highlight the key terms so you can be clear about what exactly the question wants you to do.

Revision hit list

Subject: Exam paper:

Top three target topics

Topic	What's the problem?

Next five target topics

Topic	What's the problem?

If you need to remember examples or case studies for your exam, practise using relevant information from your examples to answer different sorts of questions.

Revision hit list

Subject: Exam paper:

Top three target topics

Topic	What's the problem?

Next five target topics

Topic	What's the problem?

Examiners' report

Many of your exams will have questions where there are extra marks for SPaG. Take special care over your spelling, punctuation and grammar for these questions.

Revision hit list

Subject: Exam paper:

Top three target topics

Topic	What's the problem?

Next five target topics

Topic	What's the problem?

If you've done practice papers in your course, look back over the questions you were asked and see how you could have improved your answers.

Setting revision-session targets

A **revision session** is the time when you sit down to do **several chunks of revision**. You need short breaks between the chunks, and longer breaks between sessions.

Why should I set session targets?

If you **decide what you want to achieve** in each revision session, your revision will be more effective and you will feel more motivated.

When should I set my session targets?

It's up to you when you **decide what your targets are** for each session: it might be just before you start the session, or it might be something you plan for a day or a week.

What should my targets be?

This is up to you, too! Here are some ideas:

- Your revision hit lists are a good place to start. You could decide to tackle one problem area at the start of each session.

- You could have the target of answering a practice exam question in your session.

- You could have the target of avoiding distractions: for example, not checking your phone until a break between revision chunks.

- You could have the target of writing against the clock: giving yourself a set time to write an answer to an exam question. Knowing how much you can write in a set time is a very valuable exam skill.

Here are some tips on setting targets:

✓ Make your targets **time-specific**: decide how long you will give yourself to achieve them.

✓ Your targets should be **achievable**.

✓ Make sure your targets are **useful** for your revision.

✓ If you use the same targets each session, they could become boring. Throw in some **variety** – even some unusual targets once in a while! (But still useful, of course.)

✓ **Reward** yourself for achieving your targets!

 Use this space to record different ideas for revision-session targets.

Being objective about your thoughts means testing them to see if they are really true – a bit like a scientist carrying out an experiment.

Using the revision planner

Now you are ready to use all the information you've put together to start planning your revision sessions. You will use the **planner** section of this book (pages 59–90) for this.

IMPORTANT: We've included plenty of **planner** pages, which may be more than you need. You can use these pages to plan revision for mock exams, too.

What's the point of planning revision sessions?

You know from your revision wall chart what exam papers you are revising for each day, so why do you need to plan each session too? Planning what you will do in each revision session is useful because it helps you:

- cover everything you need for each paper – starting with the problem areas
- know what topics to revise each day
- stay focused on your targets for each session.

Many people find it easier to plan their revision sessions for a week at a time. This gives you more flexibility than planning for months in advance.

What is the difference between your wall chart and the planner?

What exam papers you are revising for each day

Details of what you are going to revise in each session

57

Getting started

Here are some tips on using the **planner** section to plan your revision sessions.

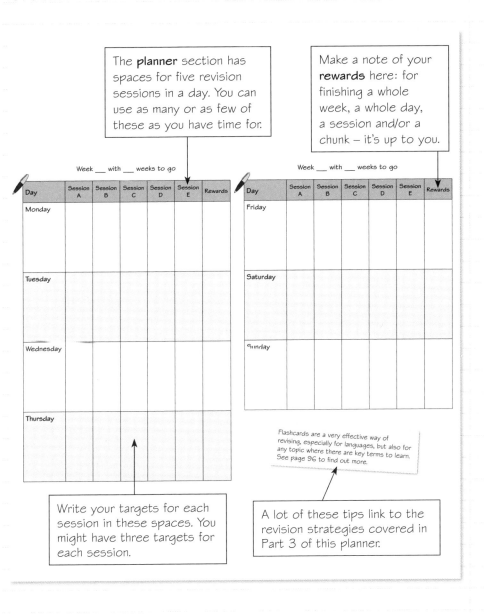

The **planner** section has spaces for five revision sessions in a day. You can use as many or as few of these as you have time for.

Make a note of your **rewards** here: for finishing a whole week, a whole day, a session and/or a chunk – it's up to you.

Week ___ with ___ weeks to go

Day	Session A	Session B	Session C	Session D	Session E	Rewards
Monday						
Tuesday						
Wednesday						
Thursday						

Week ___ with ___ weeks to go

Day	Session A	Session B	Session C	Session D	Session E	Rewards
Friday						
Saturday						
Sunday						

Flashcards are a very effective way of revising, especially for languages, but also for any topic where there are key terms to learn. See page 96 to find out more.

Write your targets for each session in these spaces. You might have three targets for each session.

A lot of these tips link to the revision strategies covered in Part 3 of this planner.

Week ___ with ___ weeks to go

Day	Session A	Session B	Session C	Session D	Session E	Rewards
Monday						
Tuesday						
Wednesday						
Thursday						

Week ___ with ___ weeks to go

Day	Session A	Session B	Session C	Session D	Session E	Rewards
Friday						
Saturday						
Sunday						

Keep yourself motivated with a reward when you hit your revision targets.

Week ___ with ___ weeks to go

Day	Session A	Session B	Session C	Session D	Session E	Rewards
Monday						
Tuesday						
Wednesday						
Thursday						

Week ___ with ___ weeks to go

Day	Session A	Session B	Session C	Session D	Session E	Rewards
Friday						
Saturday						
Sunday						

If some of your subjects have got options to them, check with your teachers to make sure you are revising the right option choices.

Week ___ with ___ weeks to go

Day	Session A	Session B	Session C	Session D	Session E	Rewards
Monday						
Tuesday						
Wednesday						
Thursday						

Week ___ with ___ weeks to go

Day	Session A	Session B	Session C	Session D	Session E	Rewards
Friday						
Saturday						
Sunday						

Take the time you need to read exam questions very carefully. Make sure you know exactly what each exam question is asking you to do before you start writing your answer.

Week ___ with ___ weeks to go

Day	Session A	Session B	Session C	Session D	Session E	Rewards
Monday						
Tuesday						
Wednesday						
Thursday						

Week ___ with ___ weeks to go

Day	Session A	Session B	Session C	Session D	Session E	Rewards
Friday						
Saturday						
Sunday						

Flow charts are a great way to remember the stages of a process. They are particularly useful in science subjects, but you can use them in lots of other subjects too. See page 97.

Week ___ with ___ weeks to go

Day	Session A	Session B	Session C	Session D	Session E	Rewards
Monday						
Tuesday						
Wednesday						
Thursday						

Week ___ with ___ weeks to go

Day	Session A	Session B	Session C	Session D	Session E	Rewards
Friday						
Saturday						
Sunday						

One of the best ways to revise for an exam is to practise answering questions from previous papers. Ask your subject teachers to help you find good questions to practise.

Week ___ with ___ weeks to go

Day	Session A	Session B	Session C	Session D	Session E	Rewards
Monday						
Tuesday						
Wednesday						
Thursday						

Week ___ with ___ weeks to go

Day	Session A	Session B	Session C	Session D	Session E	Rewards
Friday						
Saturday						
Sunday						

Your exams are likely to be spread out over a few weeks. You can keep revising in between exams, but remember to get plenty of rest too, as having lots of exams is very tiring.

Week ___ with ___ weeks to go

Day	Session A	Session B	Session C	Session D	Session E	Rewards
Monday						
Tuesday						
Wednesday						
Thursday						

Week ___ with ___ weeks to go

Day	Session A	Session B	Session C	Session D	Session E	Rewards
Friday						
Saturday						
Sunday						

If you used the revision hit list idea on pages 25–54 of this book, don't forget to keep coming back to those tricky topics in your revision.

Week ___ with ___ weeks to go

Day	Session A	Session B	Session C	Session D	Session E	Rewards
Monday						
Tuesday						
Wednesday						
Thursday						

Week ___ with ___ weeks to go

Day	Session A	Session B	Session C	Session D	Session E	Rewards
Friday						
Saturday						
Sunday						

Concept mapping is a great way to help your brain make connections to the information you need for your exams. Find out more on page 97.

Week ___ with ___ weeks to go

Day	Session A	Session B	Session C	Session D	Session E	Rewards
Monday						
Tuesday						
Wednesday						
Thursday						

Week ___ with ___ weeks to go

Day	Session A	Session B	Session C	Session D	Session E	Rewards
Friday						
Saturday						
Sunday						

It's important to review your revision as you go along. What sorts of revision techniques are working best? What do you understand now that you didn't before you started revising?

Week ___ with ___ weeks to go

Day	Session A	Session B	Session C	Session D	Session E	Rewards
Monday						
Tuesday						
Wednesday						
Thursday						

Week ___ with ___ weeks to go

Day	Session A	Session B	Session C	Session D	Session E	Rewards
Friday						
Saturday						
Sunday						

Condensing your notes into flashcards is a really good way to streamline lots of information, and put it in a way that makes it easy to test yourself. Find out more on page 96.

Week ___ with ___ weeks to go

Day	Session A	Session B	Session C	Session D	Session E	Rewards
Monday						
Tuesday						
Wednesday						
Thursday						

Week ___ with ___ weeks to go

Day	Session A	Session B	Session C	Session D	Session E	Rewards
Friday						
Saturday						
Sunday						

It's a good idea to start your revision with a topic you find challenging. You'll feel a sense of achievement, and you may be able to remember more when your brain is fresh.

Week ___ with ___ weeks to go

Day	Session A	Session B	Session C	Session D	Session E	Rewards
Monday						
Tuesday						
Wednesday						
Thursday						

Week ___ with ___ weeks to go

Day	Session A	Session B	Session C	Session D	Session E	Rewards
Friday						
Saturday						
Sunday						

It's a good idea to revise in chunks of time: probably around 20–25 minutes per chunk. Try not to get distracted. Focus on your revision then have at least a 5-minute break before the next chunk.

Week ___ with ___ weeks to go

Day	Session A	Session B	Session C	Session D	Session E	Rewards
Monday						
Tuesday						
Wednesday						
Thursday						

Week ___ with ___ weeks to go

Day	Session A	Session B	Session C	Session D	Session E	Rewards
Friday						
Saturday						
Sunday						

Just reading and re-reading your notes may not be the best way to revise. Use memory strategies to process information into something you find easy to remember. See page 95 for help with this.

Week ___ with ___ weeks to go

Day	Session A	Session B	Session C	Session D	Session E	Rewards
Monday						
Tuesday						
Wednesday						
Thursday						

Week ___ with ___ weeks to go

Day	Session A	Session B	Session C	Session D	Session E	Rewards
Friday						
Saturday						
Sunday						

Student tip For my Spanish exam, I wrote down some key topics, and then wrote advantages and disadvantages in Spanish. I find my mind can go blank in an exam, so it really helped me to do this thinking first!

Week ___ with ___ weeks to go

Day	Session A	Session B	Session C	Session D	Session E	Rewards
Monday						
Tuesday						
Wednesday						
Thursday						

Week ___ with ___ weeks to go

Day	Session A	Session B	Session C	Session D	Session E	Rewards
Friday						
Saturday						
Sunday						

Taking a short amount of time at the end of each day to quickly review what you've covered can work really well. You can also start each day's revision by recapping what you did the previous day.

Week ___ with ___ weeks to go

Day	Session A	Session B	Session C	Session D	Session E	Rewards
Monday						
Tuesday						
Wednesday						
Thursday						

Week ___ with ___ weeks to go

Day	Session A	Session B	Session C	Session D	Session E	Rewards
Friday						
Saturday						
Sunday						

Flashcards are a very effective way of revising, especially for languages, but also for any topic where there are key terms to learn. See page 96 to find out more.

Reviewing your revision

You have reached the end of Part 2. In the same way as you reviewed your revision wall chart at the end of Part 1, you should now review your Revision Planner.

✓ Look quickly through your revision checklists and hit lists.

✓ Reflect on how organised you are now for your revision, and how much this will help you do well – which it really will!

✓ Think ahead to challenging topics and days when it might be hard to get motivated. Consider some tactics you could use to help you keep going.

Making time to review your revision as you start and finish each session is a very effective revision technique. Here are some questions you could use to focus your 5-minute reviews:

? What do I know now that I didn't know (or remember) at the start of the session?

? How does what I've revised today link to what I've already covered for this subject?

? Based on what I've revised today, what do I think I should revise next?

? Thinking about the way I revised, what strategies worked best for me?

? Is there anything I could change about the way I revise to make it more effective?

? How would I summarise what I've covered this session in five points?

Space for reflection

Use this space to record your thoughts on your revision. Make a note of the:

- challenges so far
- challenges ahead
- ways you are going to tackle the challenges.

Part 3: Revision strategies

Part 3 gives you a quick guide to some tried-and-tested revision strategies.

Revision strategies make your revision:
- ✓ more effective (you learn more and learn better)
- ✓ more varied (less boring)
- ✓ easier and quicker.

It should take about 30 minutes to read through this section.

Understanding revision

Your brain learns best when you ask it to **make connections and create meanings**. This means that unpicking information, explaining it to yourself and (especially) applying your knowledge in new ways is a very effective way to revise.

Reading information through is not as effective. You might remember it for a few seconds, but your brain won't keep hold of much of it.

Pick and mix

Not all these revision strategies will work for you, and some will be better for some subjects than others. If you get stuck with revising a topic in one way, try out another strategy to see if that helps.

To test out a revision strategy, try it and then test how much you remember a) immediately after the revision and then b) the next day.

If you've been successful in making connections and creating your own meanings in your revision, then it is much more likely that you will have succeeded in moving information to long-term memory. Your long-term memory is what you'll rely on in your exams.

Condensing your notes

Condensing your notes means making **summaries of the main points**. Why is this a good idea?

✓ Making the summaries is good revision.

✓ The summaries are a lot easier to revise from.

There are **four steps** to condensing your notes:

1 Get your notes organised (see page 21). You may choose to highlight key points as you go through.

2 For each page of your notes, write a summary of the main points on a piece of paper.

3 Condense each summary down to the main ideas, key terms and key points.

4 Write your condensed notes on index cards, leaving plenty of space between points.

Worked example

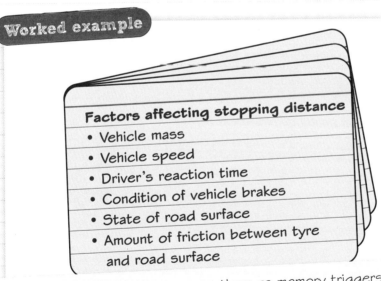

Factors affecting stopping distance
- Vehicle mass
- Vehicle speed
- Driver's reaction time
- Condition of vehicle brakes
- State of road surface
- Amount of friction between tyre and road surface

Condensing notes helps you use them as memory triggers for recalling the details of a topic, its key issues and the evidence that you will need to answer fully in your exam.

Memory strategies

Memory strategies are **tried-and-tested ways of helping your brain remember things**. There are lots of different methods. Here are three of the best:

First-letter phrases

Use the first letters of a list of things you need to remember to make up a **memorable phrase**.

For example, here are six types of hard-engineering coastal defences: **r**ip-rap, **s**eawalls, **r**evetments, **o**ffshore reefs, **g**roynes, **g**abions. The first letters could make up the phrase: *Rip Saws Really Open Great Gaps*.

Putting things in your own words

Read your notes, then turn the page over and see how much of the information you can write down.

Now read your notes, and **explain what they mean to someone else**, or just out loud to yourself. Turn your notes over and see how much you can recall this time. It should be more.

Make unusual connections

Your brain locks on to things that seem unusual. Try thinking of **weird connections** to things you need to remember. For example, if you had to remember that Patrick Manson discovered the spread of disease by mosquitoes, you could imagine a man and his son running from a huge mosquito.

Student tip Use your imagination! For example, I drew long hydrocarbons with **lots** of weak forces between molecules, which made it easier to remember why they were difficult to separate – and so had high boiling points.

Flashcards

Flashcards are often used in Languages because they are great for testing yourself on vocabulary. You could use them for testing yourself on key terms in lots of other subjects, too.

Flashcards have something to remember on one side of a card, and the explanation or definition on the other; you can make them using card or paper. It can also be useful to make a presentation, with the first slide of a pair being the thing you need to revise and the next slide being the answer.

Successful revision strategy sequence

Combine approaches for a **revision 'power-up'**:

✓ Condense your notes.

✓ Explain your summaries to someone else.

✓ Make flashcards from your summary points.

✓ Test yourself using your flashcards.

A lot of people use highlighter pens to identify things they need to remember in their notes. This doesn't really engage your brain in making connections so it isn't always a very effective way of revising.

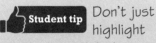 **Student tip** Don't just highlight or rewrite points in your notes – make sure you really understand them first. You can't revise something you don't really understand in the first place!

 Student tip I would read a section in my Revision Guide, make sure I understood it, and then write it down as concisely as I could in my own revision notes. I found actually writing it helped me learn it – it made revising from my notes much easier, as I had everything I needed there!

Getting visual

Drawing diagrams and using pictures to help you revise works really well.

Flow charts

These are good for revising **processes**. For example, a product life cycle in Design and Technology:

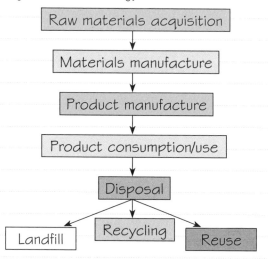

Concept maps

Concept maps are a good way of revising **how one thing connects to something else**. A good technique is to start one as you start revising a new topic and map the connections as you go through. Once it is done, hide it and try to redraw it.

Tips for good concept maps

1 Use a **big piece of paper** – A3 size – or do your map on screen so you've plenty of room to expand.

2 Use **different colours** for the different branches of your map.

3 Use **pictures** (unusual ones if possible) in your map to help you remember it.

97

Past papers and mark schemes

What are past papers and mark schemes?

Past papers are **old exam papers**. Mark schemes are guidelines on what marks examiners should give for different kinds of answers.

Why use past papers for revision?

Trying out older versions of the exams you will be sitting is brilliant practice because:

- you get to know how your exams work
- you get a chance to try out what you know with real questions
- you can find out how to improve your answers
- you get to understand what your examiners are looking for.

How do mark schemes work?

Mark schemes can be very simple for some questions – they give the right answer or answers. For longer questions they are trickier though: ask your teacher for help. Exam boards sometimes have model answers on their websites, and these are useful too.

Where can I find past papers and mark schemes?

On your exam board's websites, but because exams change quite often, it is best to ask your teachers for past papers and mark schemes so you use the right ones for your courses.

You could also take a look at the Practice Papers Plus series, available for a range of subjects. These offer further exam-style practice, along with fully worked solutions to help you understand how to tackle questions step by step.

Understanding exam questions

There are lots of different types of exam question, but there are three main steps to answering all of them.

1 Read the question **very carefully.**

2 Underline the **command term**(s).

3 Use the **marks** available to **plan** your answer.

What are command terms?

These are words in the question that tell you what to do. Here are some common ones and what they mean.

Outline	Give the key points but don't go into detail.
Describe	Give a detailed account of something.
Explain	Set out a detailed account that includes reasons and results, and causes and effects.
Compare	Identify the similarities and differences between things in a balanced way.
Evaluate	Work out the value of something by weighing up its strengths and its limitations.

How do I plan my answer?

The marks for the question will show you roughly how many points to make (about 1 per mark) and how long to spend on it (about 1 minute per mark). That is a **rough** guide!

Student tip If you are not sure how you will be marked, have a look at the model answers and examiners' reports available from your exam board. These will help you understand where others have gone wrong, so you don't make the same mistakes!

Understanding exam questions

Usually, the questions that are worth the most marks on an exam paper involve **extended answers** – that means answers where you have to write quite a lot to explain your thinking.

In addition to the three main steps on the previous page, here are three more tips for dealing with extended answer questions.

4 Keep your answer **relevant** to the question.

5 **Connect** your points together with linking terms.

6 Use **paragraphs**: they help to give your answer a clear structure.

Stay relevant

Every point you make should be **answering the question**. This is why it is so important to make sure you really understand what the question is asking, rather than plunging in and writing whatever you can remember about the topic. Keep referring back to the question throughout your answer.

Linking terms

Some students' answers are a mess of points all tangled together. You can avoid this by using links like 'Another reason is...' or 'However...' They signpost where your argument is going.

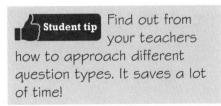
Student tip Find out from your teachers how to approach different question types. It saves a lot of time!

Top exam tips

Here are some top exam tips from students who did well in their GCSEs:

If you can, start your revision as early as possible. You need time to go over topics two or three times.

Get plenty of sleep the night before an exam.

Get lots of past papers, and work through them and use the mark schemes to see what you got right and what you could have done better.

If you've got big exams at the start of your exam time, then don't just revise for them. You need to do revision for the later exams too.

I stuck post-its with key words on them all round the house so everywhere I went I was revising!

Don't be frightened to ask your teachers for help – they'll be really glad to help you all they can.

The Easter holidays are your prime revision time: make sure you use that time to get serious about your revision.

Test yourself – there are lots of good quizzes online, for example. The best way to really find out if you remember a topic is to do a practice exam question on it.

Be prepared – exam day reminders

✓ Make sure you know **when** and **where** your exam is taking place.

✓ Aim to get to school **at least 15 minutes before** your exam starts, in case of any transport problems. There will be a seating plan to show you where you are sitting in the exam room or hall.

✓ It can get **hot** in exam halls in summer: bring **a bottle of water** with you and don't dress too warmly! Note: if your bottle has a label on it, you will have to remove that before you can take it into exams.

✓ Bring a couple of black pens to the exam: you need to write in black ink and it is good to have **a spare pen** in case one runs out. Erasable pens and gel pens are not allowed.

✓ Bring pencils, a rubber and a ruler with you. Use a **ruler** for **straight lines** in diagrams.

✓ You can bring a calculator into an exam unless you are told you can't. However, you must clear anything stored in the calculator.

✓ You can't bring a pencil case into the exam unless it is see-through: a clear plastic bag is OK.

✓ Look at past papers for your exam subjects: the first page will list what you need to bring with you.

✓ You can't take any web-enabled device or device that can store data into the exam. This includes smartwatches as well as mobile phones, portable media players, etc.

✓ **Do not talk** to anyone in the exam hall: it is strictly forbidden. If you need help from the invigilators, put your hand up.

✓ **Read** the front of the exam paper **carefully** and fill in all the boxes correctly. The invigilators will have the information you need for this.

✓ There will be a clock in the exam hall which will definitely be correct. Use it to **keep track of time** and **plan your answers**.

✓ Take some deep breaths before your exam to help you relax.

Many students have access arrangements for exams, such as scribes or readers. Talk to the person responsible for exams at your college or school about this.

Exam stress

The human stress response is something we have evolved as a species to power us through challenging situations. Stress helps us to perform at our optimal level – our brains work faster, our reactions are sharper.

Because stress is a natural response, it is not something we can decide to have or not have. But we can **manage** our stress.

Planning for stress

Plan time to rest and relax. This is as important as planning your revision sessions. Check back over your revision so far. Are you getting enough sleep? Are you breaking up revision sessions with time to relax? How are you enjoying your rewards – should you be rewarding yourself more?

Worry time

Sometimes it can feel like worries go round and round in your head. Health experts recommend actually setting time aside for worrying. What you do is this:

1 Set up worry time. This is a specific time of day when you will worry about things for a specific amount of time. You have to keep your worry time appointment each day for it to work.

2 Then, whenever you start to worry about something, jot down your worry. Say, 'I will worry about this during worry time'.

3 When it is worry time, go through the list of worries you've put together that day.

You can problem solve worries in worry time: work out ways to deal with them. Some worries are hypothetical – 'what if?' sorts of worries. These are worries we can't solve and worrying about them won't be useful or helpful. These are worries we should try to let go.

Part 4: Introducing mindfulness

The mindfulness practices in this book can help you to stay calm and focused as you revise for your exams.

Important

If you feel that stress and anxiety are getting on top of you, speak to an adult that you trust. Opening up about how you feel can really help in dealing with what can be an intense time.

If you have recently experienced the loss of a loved one, a traumatic event or have been diagnosed with a mental illness, or have any ongoing physical pain, it's really important that you check in with someone (such as a parent, teacher, counsellor or doctor) before doing these practices.

What is mindfulness?

Mindfulness is a great way to help you prepare for exams. But what is it and how does it work?

Mindfulness is essentially awareness. It is about training your attention to notice your thoughts, feelings, sensations, and anything around you that is happening right now, without judging them. By doing this, you step away from automatic responses and observe what it means to be in the present with an open mind. This can help you to make better, more skilful decisions.

Your brain can be 'rewired' to work in more helpful or skilful ways. In many ways it's like brain training. Just as people go to the gym and lift weights regularly to build muscle, so mindfulness helps train the brain by doing the practices daily.

Preparing for exams

Neuroscientists are just starting to understand more about how mindfulness practice can help. Studies indicate that it helps in two main ways, especially when it comes to exams.

1 It helps to increase the density in the front of your brain. This is the part of the brain associated with **memory**, your ability to **solve problems** and to **manage distraction**.

2 It helps us to manage strong or difficult emotions. Feeling some stress and anxiety around exams is natural and, indeed, can **help boost performance**. It's when this becomes too much that it becomes a problem. Mindfulness helps to calm activity in the bit of your brain associated with worry.

The form of mindfulness that we have used in this book was developed by three psychologists: Zindel Segal, Mark Williams and John Teasdale.

Connecting mind, body, emotions and behaviour

Mindfulness isn't just about training the mind – it's also about you connecting with your emotions and your behaviour.

Emotions and feelings can affect our bodies and our actions, and vice versa. Just as thinking can affect physical reactions (for example, feeling anxious can cause 'butterflies' in the tummy before an exam), so your body can affect your thinking.

By becoming aware of emotions, you can try to deal with them before they grow too strong or start to take over your thinking. Some of the practices in this book will help you reconnect with your body.

105

Doing and being

Very often, it is easy to want to get straight into doing a task like revision just to get it finished and out of the way. This is called **doing mode** – it helps you to gets things done, but not always to consider the **best way** of tackling the task.

Mindfulness helps by giving you a moment to pause and enter **being mode**. This allows time for you to ground yourself and be fully focused on the present moment, so you experience things more fully. Usually this will help you to take a calmer and wiser approach to a task, which will mean you're more effective. The practices that you are given in this book can help you to create this mental space.

Moving into being mode

The pressures of revision and exams may make you feel that taking 'time out' from revision to do these practices is not possible. However, regularly doing even short practices where you can drop into 'being mode' can begin to give you greater mental space or clarity.

You can practise the following simple exercise to help you come out of doing mode and move into being mode, which creates a more mindful, moment-by-moment experience. It might seem a bit silly to start off with, when you're so used to doing a task without giving it much thought. However, the purpose of doing this exercise is to move away from doing things automatically and, instead, start to be fully in each moment and experience it more completely through all the senses.

Mindfully making a drink

- What can you **hear?** For example, when making a drink, notice the sound of pouring the drink or boiling water.

- What can you **smell?** For example, for tea, coffee or juice, notice how the smells **change** as you make the drink.

- What can you **see?** For example, notice the colours and how they **change**.

- What can you **feel?** For example, the warmth or coolness of a drink in your hands.

- What can you **taste?** For example, when taking a sip of drink, notice how it first tastes and any **changes** in taste.

- Enjoy **being in the moment** as you consume your drink.

This simple exercise can have a big impact. Many people find they notice and taste far more.

When you take time to slow down and live in a more moment-to-moment way, you are able to experience life more fully and appreciatively.

This can then help to create a greater sense of **calm**.

Practising mindfulness

In addition to everyday mindfulness, you can do more formal practice, which is sometimes referred to as **meditation**. Just like learning any new skill, for example playing a sport or an instrument, mindfulness is something that has to be practised daily to have richer benefits. Doing daily practices of 10 minutes or so can really help you to move your awareness to be fully in the present moment in a non-judgemental way, helping you to avoid overthinking, which can lead to worry, anxiety and stress.

Practices in this planner

This planner includes three introductory practices which are useful techniques to help ground and anchor you in the present moment and encourage you to be accepting and kind to yourself. The practices are:

- Mindfulness of Breath and Body
- The Body Scan
- The Three-Step Breathing Space

Each practice is accompanied by an audio file.

If you are interested in mindfulness, speak to your teacher to see if a course is running in your school that can give you a structured programme to follow, or search online for 'mindfulness in schools'.

Being kind to yourself

Exam preparation can be a stressful time, so it's important to take some time out regularly to be kind to yourself: to recharge your batteries, give your brain some breathing space, and acknowledge all the good preparatory work you're putting in. Take regular breaks and enjoy some 'downtime' with your friends and family to help recharge. Using the three practices regularly can also help keep you calm and focused during your revision period.

Good posture for practice

Getting your posture correct for doing mindfulness practice is really important. The practices in this planner are designed to be done in a seated position. The Body Scan can also be done lying down.

Try to find a chair you can sit in that allows your feet to rest fully on the ground with your ankles, knees and hips all at right angles, with your back slightly away from the back of the chair so you can sit upright in an alert, but not tense, manner. Being comfortable will help to reduce distraction – but don't choose a chair that's so comfy that you fall asleep!

The room you choose should be somewhere you won't be disturbed. Turn your phone onto silent or flight mode. Let the people you live with know that you'll be doing mindfulness practice so that they do not disturb you.

Mindfulness can help you take a healthy, effective approach to your revision. But remember, you will still need to plan and revise!

 Mindfulness

Practice 1: Mindfulness of Breath and Body

Very often our minds like to wander. In this practice, you focus your attention on your breathing and on different parts of your body. It's a bit like shining a torchlight so that you focus on just one thing at a time, feeling the sensations that arise. Practising this regularly helps the mind wander less, which leads to less worrying and helps with concentration. Remember – it is normal for your mind to wander while you are meditating as that is what minds do! You are just trying to train it.

If your mind wanders, try to bring it back with a sense of kindness. It doesn't matter how many times the mind wanders, it's bringing it back each time to the focus on the breath or the body that's important, as you are increasing your concentration and training your attention each time. Don't be frustrated, as it is just part of training your brain.

The **Mindfulness of Breath and Body** practice will help you to develop your awareness and focus, which can help with revision. In addition, focusing on breath also has a calming effect (great if you are worrying about exams). Moving the focus to the body can also help to identify physical feelings caused by stress. Examples of stress in the body might be 'butterflies' or cramps in your tummy, your hands shaking, getting sweaty, or your mouth going dry.

To access the audio file for Practice 1, please scan the QR code or visit http://activetea.ch/32wQnxo

 Mindfulness

Practice 2: The Body Scan

Just as thoughts and emotions can affect our bodies, stress and tension in the body can affect our thinking and our feelings.

Constant analysis of problems (such as worrying about exams) can be exhausting and doesn't really help to find a solution. Sensing what's going on in your body can help to reduce the amount of time you spend analysing your problems. It grounds you back into your body, allowing you to see where you might be holding emotions and feelings as stress/tension in different parts of the body.

In the **Body Scan** practice, you move attention to different areas of the body, which allows you to feel where you might be holding emotions, such as worry. As you hold each different part of your body in awareness, really explore what feelings or sensations are arising in each one. This can help you to move away from thinking or analysing your problems too much. It can also improve posture, which, in turn, can improve thinking.

This practice can be done either lying down or sitting down. If you're lying down then find somewhere comfortable but not so comfortable you might fall asleep!

To access the audio file for Practice 2, please scan the QR code or visit http://activetea.ch/306mG4R

 **Mindfulness**

Practice 3: The Three-Step Breathing Space

Worrying about what has gone on in the past or what might happen in the future cannot change events, and distracts you from the present – from what you are doing now. The present **is** something that you can change, so that is where your focus should be. For example, worrying about your exams in several months' time won't be as helpful as revising now!

The **Three-Step Breathing Space** practice helps you to fully ground yourself in the present, and gives you a few moments to rest and recharge. The practice is structured a bit like an hourglass.

1 Firstly, you do a 'weather check' of the mind, to see what's going on, by observing your thoughts, giving you a more objective viewpoint of how busy or calm your mind is.

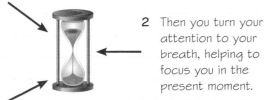

2 Then you turn your attention to your breath, helping to focus you in the present moment.

3 Finally, you expand out that awareness to sensations in the rest of your body, becoming aware of where you may be holding any emotions in the body as stress or tension.

The Three-Step Breathing Space is a very useful practice if ever you start to feel stressed and want a pause to help you step back and get perspective. The really great thing about this practice is that you can do it in three minutes or less. Use it to 'recharge' yourself while revising or ground yourself just before or even during your exam.

To access the audio file for Practice 3, please scan the QR code or visit http://activetea.ch/34EAMh4

Good luck
in all of
your GCSE
exams!

Notes

Published by Pearson Education Limited, 80 Strand, London, WC2R 0RL.
www.pearsonschoolsandfecolleges.co.uk

Text and original illustrations © Pearson Education Limited 2014
Typeset by QBS Learning Ltd
Illustrated by KJA Artists, John Hallett and QBS Learning Ltd
Cover illustration by Eoin Coveney

The rights of Rob Bircher and Ashley Lodge to be identified as authors of this work have been asserted by
them in accordance with the Copyright, Designs and Patents Act 1988.

First published 2014

23 22 21 20
10 9 8 7 6 5 4 3 2 1

British Library Cataloguing in Publication Data
A catalogue record for this book is available from the British Library

ISBN 978 1 292 31886 8

Photo acknowledgement

Shutterstock: AndreyCherkasov 104.

Printed in China by Golden Cup

Note from the publisher

Pearson has robust editorial processes, including answer and fact checks, to ensure the accuracy of the
content in this publication, and every effort is made to ensure this publication is free of errors. We are,
however, only human, and occasionally errors do occur. Pearson is not liable for any misunderstandings that
arise as a result of errors in this publication, but it is our priority to ensure that the content is accurate. If
you spot an error, please do contact us at resourcescorrections@pearson.com so we can make sure it is
corrected.